MY VACATION
DRAWING
BOOK

by Gillian Johnson

ACKNOWLEDGEMENTS

Publishing Director	Piers Pickard
Art Director	Andy Mansfield
Commissioning Editors	Jen Feroze,
	Catharine Robertson
Author and illustrator	Gillian Johnson
Editor	Jacqueline McCann
Print Production	Larissa Frost,
	Nigel Longuet
With thanks to	Jennifer Dixon

Published in April 2018 by Lonely Planet Global Limited
CRN 554153
ISBN 978 1 78701 317 9
www.lonelyplanetkids.com
© Lonely Planet 2018

10 9 8 7 6 5 4 3 2 1

Printed in China

Lonely Planet Offices

Australia
The Malt Store, Level 3, 551 Swanston St., Carlton,
Victoria 3053
T: 03 8379 8000

Ireland
Digital Depot, Roe Lane (off Thomas St), Digital Hub, Dublin 8,
D08 TCV4

USA
124 Linden St., Oakland, CA 94607
T: 510 250 64.00

UK
240 Blackfriars Rd., London SE1 8NW
T: 020 3771 5100

STAY IN TOUCH
lonelyplanet.com/contact

MY VACATION
DRAWING
BOOK

CALLING
ALL
TRAVELERS!

There is no right way to draw — everyone has their own style, and one person's mistake is another person's masterpiece. Follow our easy tips, and you'll come home with a book packed with sketches and doodles that will help you relive your amazing vacation.

MY VACATION

Let's start with you — that's a good place! Where are you going? Who's going with you? Fill in the empty boxes with words, doodles, drawings, and whatever you feel like.

This is me!

Where I live...

Where I'm going...

Who's going with me...

MK, me, dad

How I'll get there...

airplane

Most looking forward to...

swimming

WHAT YOU NEED

Wherever you find yourself, you'll need a few drawing tools, such as pencils, markers, crayons, and pastels. A water soluble marker is great for smearing, blending, and creating special effects. An eraser and pencil sharpener are also useful. Keep all your pens together in a pencil case and store it in your backpack for easy access. You're all set!

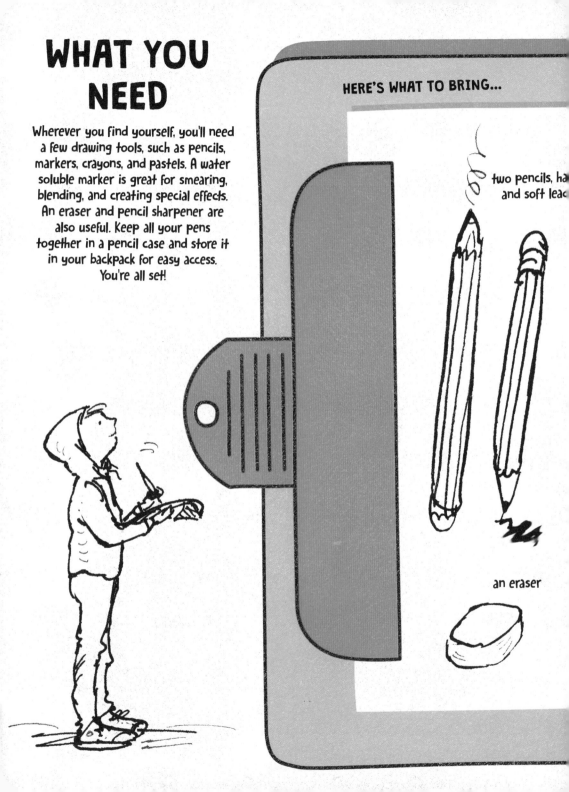

HERE'S WHAT TO BRING...

two pencils, ha
and soft lead

an eraser

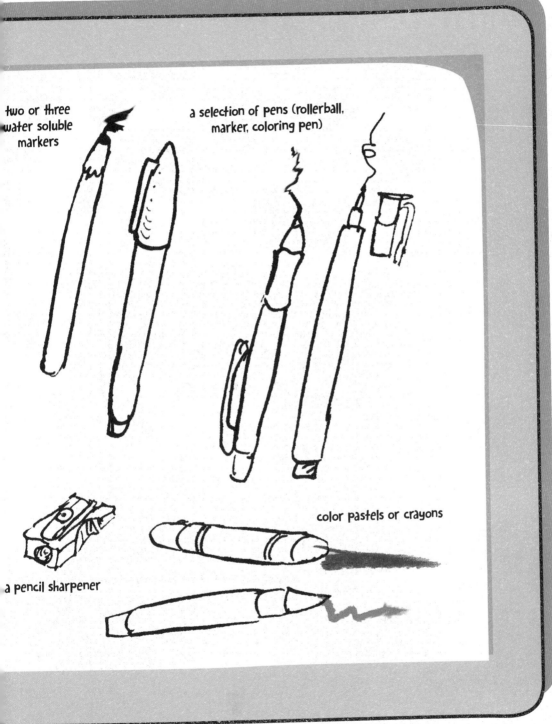

two or three
water soluble
markers

a selection of pens (rollerball,
marker, coloring pen)

color pastels or crayons

a pencil sharpener

WARM UP

You don't need to be an art ace to draw what you see, just be prepared to have fun on the page. With a few pens, pencils, an eraser, and some water, you can create amazing effects. Choose your pen, and see what it can do. Don't worry about being messy – it's important to experiment!

Lines

Lines can be long, short, straight, squiggly, thick, or thin.

Take a line for a walk...

Continue these patterns across the space.

Scribbles

Scribbles don't have to have any structure at all. Just let loose!

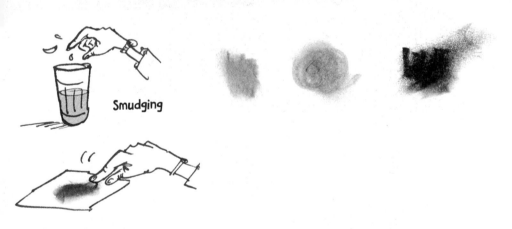

Smudging

Dip your finger in water to smudge and blur pen and pencil lines.

LET GO

Fill this page with balloons! Who was holding them before they escaped?

WHERE TO?

Where are you going? Write the names of the places you'll visit on your journey on the signpost.

Decorate the sign HOWEVER you like! try a mix of CAPITAL And lowercase Letters and use different colors.

Draw a map showing how you get to your destination. Use your imagination, and show some of the things you might pass along the way.

TOP TIP

Make a map key. You could include features such as a house, town, lake, forest, mountain, train station, airport, hospital, and school. Can you think of others?

BUBBLE LETTERS

All packed? Make sure your suitcase or backpack has your name on it. Create your own personalized baggage tag using bubble letters.

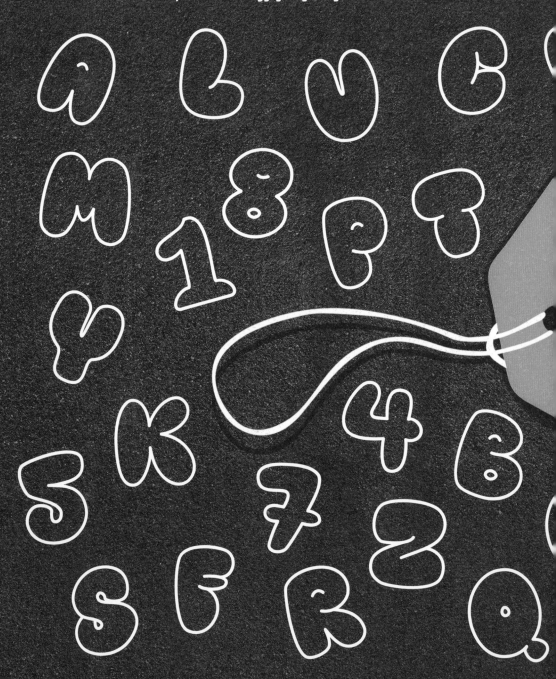

NAME

ADDRESS

COUNTRY

TELEPHONE

STICK PEOPLE

Who is going with you? Your mom, dad, sister, or brother? Classmates on a school trip? Try to capture them as stick people. They work best if their actions seem real. Group a few stick people together, and before you know it, you'll have a story.

Draw some happy stick figures. Try to make the head and body the same length as the legs.

Draw sad stick figures. Think about the angles of the body and head to get the emotions across.

Sketch angry stick figures! The elbows are halfway down the arms and point backwards. Knees are halfway down the legs and point forwards.

Now draw exhausted stick figures, and see if you can copy the angles of their poses.

MY STICK FAMILY PORTRAIT

Test your stick-drawing technique by applying it to your own family. Try to capture your family when they are hanging around. Use speech bubbles to add funny comments!

It's your turn! Maybe you're at an airport, or train station, or about to board a ferry? See if you can recreate the scene using simple stick people and speech bubbles. Add a caption, too.

TAKE A CLOSE LOOK

Many of the objects that you see around you can be broken down into simple shapes. Most objects can be broken down into a sphere, cube, or cylinder – the building blocks of drawing. Whenever you draw, it helps to look for these basic shapes.

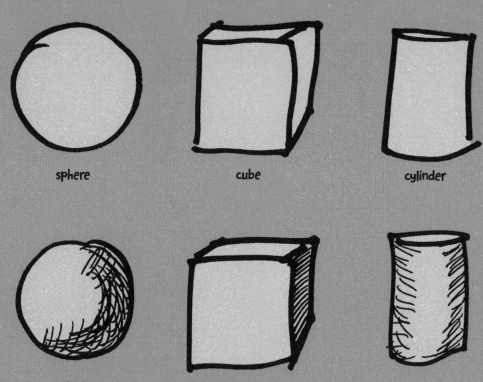

sphere   cube   cylinder

Adding little lines with a fine pen will help to make objects appear 3-D.

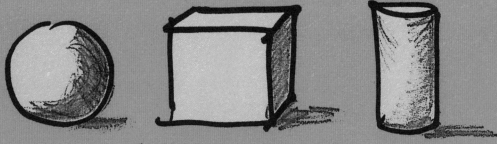

With a pencil, you can create a soft shadow.

Practice drawing these shapes. Then, using a fine black pen, add lines to create a 3-D appearance. Finally, use your pencil to add shading and depth.

...EVEN CLOSER

The cube, sphere, and cylinder form the basic shape for all kinds of everyday objects, and even people. Learn to look for these shapes.

cubes

spheres

cylinders

faces

Can you turn these shapes into everyday objects?

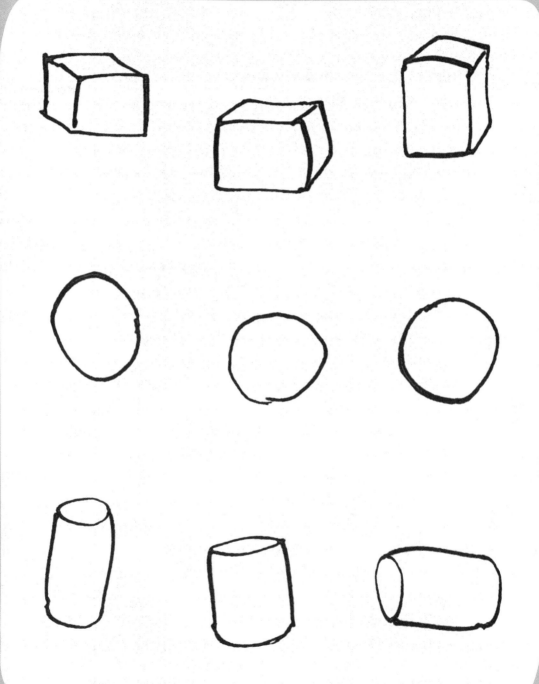

CRAZY CREATURES

Can you change these basic shapes into animals? Feel free to go a little crazy. We've done a few for you!

ON THE MOVE

Whether you're camping with a friend from school, on a train to go and visit Grandma, or hopping on a plane to Timbuktu, you'll need a vehicle of some kind to get you there. Have a go at drawing yours, and remember to look for the basic shapes that make up vehicles!

THE HORIZON

The place where the land meets the sky is called the horizon. On the page, it looks like a straight line drawn across the middle. It can be high up, low down, wavy, bumpy, straight, or pointed.

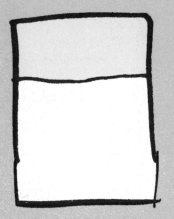

Draw your horizon high up. This will give you space for details in the foreground and less room for sky.

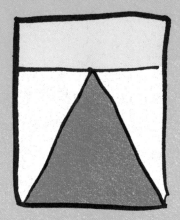

Draw two lines from the foreground to the middle of the horizon to create a road disappearing into the distance.

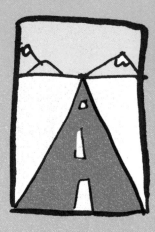

Add details such as mountains in the distance. Experiment with making them higher or lower.

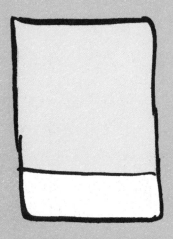

A lower horizon line gives a bigger sky but leaves less room for foreground detail.

Now add a series of lines getting smaller and smaller to create utility poles.

Add a few road markings, some fluffy clouds, or W shapes for birds in the sky.

It's your turn. Experiment by drawing a horizon that is high up the page. Add a few simple details to your scene to create a landscape.

Now draw a horizon that is lower down the page.

VANISHING POINT

When something is so far away and so small, it seems to vanish. That's the vanishing point! When you're trying to add depth (called perspective) to your drawings, it helps to remember that things that are far away look much smaller than things that are close up.

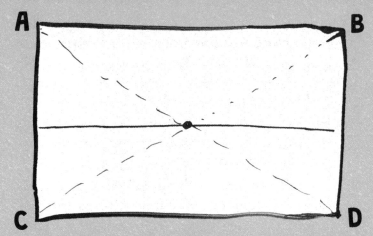

A page with a horizon line, a vanishing point, and dotted lines connecting the two will help you create a drawing with perspective.

The bigger buildings and trees in this picture appear closer. Smaller trees and buildings seem far away.

Now it's your turn to experiment with perspective. Draw your horizon and vanishing point and connect them with faint lines.

A

B

C

D

Try drawing simple buildings, trees, or utility poles to create a scene with perspective.

PERSPECTIVE

Have a go at drawing people using perspective.
The same rule applies: the smaller you draw them,
the further away they will appear! What
are your people doing?

When you're lined up for a race, you'll notice that the boy standing
next to you looks much bigger than the boy standing farthest away!

These skiers are ready for a downhill challenge. Change a few details and positions to give the impression that your people are all different.

MARK-MAKING

When you add lines, flecks, specks, dots, crisscrosses, and bubbles, it adds texture to your sketches and drawings.

Practice making marks here. Can you think of other marks you can make?
Think about how you can apply marks like these to your sketches.

LIGHT & SHADE

Shadows happen when light hits the object you are drawing. To figure out how to draw shadows, imagine pointing a flashlight at the thing you're drawing. The shadows happen in the places the light doesn't reach.

If you have a flashlight, shine it on an object and see where the shadow falls.

What happens to the shadow when you shine the flashlight from above or below?

Using a soft pencil, add your shadow lightly, then smudge. Don't make it too dark.

Shadows can create a scary atmosphere!

It's your turn. Add shadows to these sketches and think carefully about how the light from the flashlight will hit each one. Where will the shadows fall?

TREES AND MORE TREES

No matter where you are, it's very likely there will be trees (unless you're on the moon). First, try to capture the general shape – is it round, oval, triangular? Don't worry about adding individual leaves. Where is the light coming from? Add shadows.

oval / round

three circles

triangular

Have a go at drawing tree shapes. You could add branches — they are thicker at the base than at the tip. Then add markings and create shadows using a soft pencil.

DRAW A FOREST

Draw different tree shapes and create a forest. Add leaves at the top to make a leafy canopy. Think about basic shapes, and have a go at branches. They are like veins, getting smaller and smaller as they reach towards the sky. Let the branches curve a little, too. Add markings to your tree trunks and canopy. Have fun, and remember – there are no mistakes!

CONTOUR DRAWING

Contour drawing is a classic art exercise. Try not to look at your pencil or paper as you draw – so you are drawing "blind." Look at an object and try to imagine that your pen is almost touching the edge as you outline it (*contour* is French for "outline"). Let's start with the hand. Don't peek!

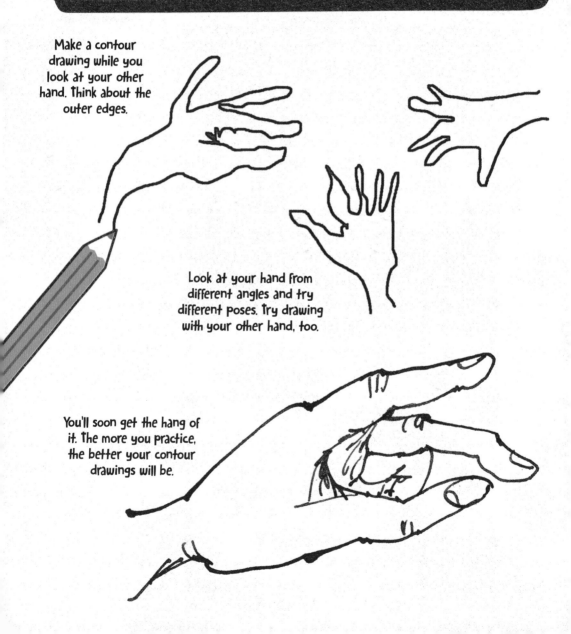

Make a contour drawing while you look at your other hand. Think about the outer edges.

Look at your hand from different angles and try different poses. Try drawing with your other hand, too.

You'll soon get the hang of it. The more you practice, the better your contour drawings will be.

Use this space to practice sketching your own hand.
Don't worry if it looks a bit messy to start – that's the idea!

A IS FOR ACCOMMODATION

Where are you staying on your vacation? What's it like? Are you in a skyscraper 50 floors up? Sleeping in a campervan or a tent? Whether you're in a hotel, tree house, or at sea, try recreating the place where you are laying your head! Zzzzzzzzz.

LOOK UP!

If you're in a town or a city, take a few moments to look up – what do you see? Does the skyline look different from the one where you live? Draw a row of tall rectangles, and then draw another row in front to create a sense of depth, or perspective.

TOP TIP

Add lots of details to your rectangles – dots, dashes, or squares to look like windows. Work on your roof shapes and try to make them different.

GRAND FACADE

When you look closely at a skyline, individual buildings such as museums, palaces, and churches may be very grand. Use a soft pencil to sketch a grand building – or your favorite building.

Use your finger to rub and smudge your image slightly.

With a fine black pen, add a few details to bring your building to life.

Try to recreate a building you have seen on your travels, or one close to where you live.

Experiment with a fine black pen and practice your mark-making skills to bring your building to life.

PEOPLE, PEOPLE, PEOPLE

It's a lot of fun watching people, with a pen in one hand and a sketchbook in the other. Whether you're strolling through town, throwing a frisbee on the beach, or walking in the woods, try to capture something of the people around you.

People move, so you need to work quickly! Try to capture a general shape. It might take a few people before you get the hang of it, but don't worry – you'll get better the more you try.

TOP TIP

Let loose! Dab a few fingerprints on the page and you can turn those into people, too!

DRAWING FACES

Round, oval, egg-shaped, or square – heads and faces come in all shapes and sizes! Here are a few handy tips to remember when you're drawing them.

1 Draw an egg-shaped face to begin.

2 Sketch the eyes about halfway up. There should be a lot of space above the eyes.

3 The tips of the ears begin just a little above the eyes and end halfway between the eyes and the chin.

4 The nose sits at the same level as the ends of the ears.

5 The bottom lip sits halfway between the bottom of the earlobes and the chin. The mouth is shaped a little like a wide triangle!

Now you have a go. Try using a combination of pencils: a thick crayon or pastel for hair and a thinner black pen for details.

MOODY PEOPLE

You can create a range of moods by altering the shape of the mouth or the eyes. Varying the distance between the eyes changes someone a lot. Have a go, and then write funny captions to show how the people are feeling.

HATS OFF

Hats can completely change a person's appearance. Like people, each hat has its own personality. Have a little fun adding your own hats to the people here – or copy one that's around the edge of the page. Do the hats suit their wearers?

BIRDS

Take a moment to notice the different kinds of birds around you. Even if you're not in a place filled with feathered friends, this bird drill will help you to draw them anywhere!

The basic shape is the most important part of making a bird look like a bird!

A bird shape is a series of circles, ovals, triangles, and cylinders.

Add details such as feathers and feet, a pointy beak, a beady eye, and tail feathers.

Use this space for your bird studies.

CREATURES GREAT AND SMALL

The world is full of beautiful beasts. Lizards on walls, ants marching by the pool, dogs sleeping in the shade, horses in the field, birds in the sky, or whales in the sea... See if you can outline them here - practice your contour drawing.

CREATE A MENU

One of the great things about being on vacation is that you get to try all kinds of new things and eat all sorts of treats. Create the perfect menu of all your favorite things from your trip using your best swirly lettering.

STREET SIGNS

Have you seen any interesting street signs on your journey? Lots of countries have signs that might seem strange to you. Here are a few. Why not draw one you have seen, or make one up for fun!

AT THE BEACH

Head down to the beach and record what you see. Or imagine what you might see!
Try to use some of the techniques you've learned so far.

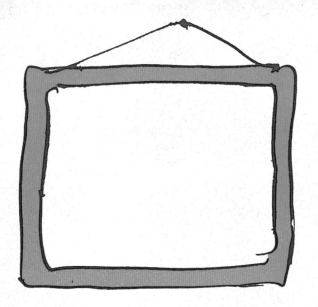

PICTURE GALLERY

If you could frame the most incredible things you've done so far on your vacation, what would they be? Mountain climbing, zip-lining, swimming, playing soccer, riding a horse, or climbing a tree?

Or why not ask everyone to empty their pockets and draw the things that most remind you of your trip!

SAY GOODBYE

Now you know that cool things can happen on the page with a few simple techniques and a little practice. What have you enjoyed sketching most? Here's a place to show off!